SPOTLIGHT ON
IMMIGRATION AND MIGRATION

THE TRANSATLANTIC SLAVE TRADE

THE FORCED MIGRATION OF AFRICANS TO AMERICA (1607–1830)

Richard Alexander

PowerKiDS press™

NEW YORK

Published in 2016 by The Rosen Publishing Group, Inc.
29 East 21st Street, New York, NY 10010

Editor: Katie Kawa
Book Design: Samantha DeMartin / Laura Bowen

Photo Credits: Cover, p. 22 Everett Historical/Shutterstock.com; p. 5 De Agostini Picture Library/ Getty Images; pp. 6, 16 MPI/Archive Photos/Getty Images; pp. 7, 9, 20 Hulton Archive/ Getty Images; p. 8 DEA/A. DAGLI ORTI/De Agostini/Getty Images; p. 10 Frederic Lewis/Archive Photos/ Getty Images; p. 11 DEA/G. DAGLI ORTI/De Agostini Picture Library/Getty Images; pp. 12, 15 Universal History Archive/Universal Images Group/Getty Images; p. 13 Print Collector/Hulton Archive/ Getty Images; p. 17 (Douglass) Fastfission~commonswiki/Wikimedia Commons; p. 17 (Jacobs) Josette/ Wikimedia Commons; pp. 18–19 PhotoQuest/Archive Photos/Getty Images; p. 21 courtesy of the Library of Congress.

Library of Congress Cataloging-in-Publication Data

Alexander, Richard.
The transatlantic slave trade : the forced migration of Africans to America (1607-1830) / Richard Alexander.
    pages cm — (Spotlight on immigration and migration)
 Includes index.
 ISBN 978-1-5081-4100-6 (pbk.)
 ISBN 978-1-5081-4101-3 (6 pack)
 ISBN 978-1-5081-4103-7 (library binding)
1. Slave trade—America—History—Juvenile literature. 2. Slave trade—Africa—History—Juvenile literature. 3. Slavery—United States—History—Juvenile literature. I. Title.
 HT1049.A42 2016
 306.3′620973—dc23
                                        2015034200

Manufactured in the United States of America

CPSIA Compliance Information: Batch #BW16PK: For further information contact Rosen Publishing, New York, New York at 1-800-237-9932.

CONTENTS

THE START OF THE SLAVE TRADE

Early **immigrants** to North America and South America came to what was called the New World for many different reasons. Some came in search of a better life or to take advantage of the many resources available. Others came for religious and political freedom. However, a large number of people didn't come to the New World by choice. Over a period of about 300 years, more than 10 million Africans were forced from their homelands to North America and South America to become slaves.

The Portuguese were the first Europeans to take slaves from Africa. They and the Spanish began to bring African slaves to the Americas in the 1500s. These first African slaves were forced to work in South America and on Caribbean islands.

This **engraving** shows slaves at work in the tobacco fields on an island in the Caribbean Sea.

SLAVERY COMES TO JAMESTOWN

By the seventeenth century, European colonies in North America and South America were beginning to grow. Leaders soon discovered, though, that they didn't have enough people to work the vast areas of land they now owned. One solution was to use enslaved Africans for labor. Slaves were a popular choice for labor because their labor was free.

In 1607, English settlers reached Jamestown in what's now Virginia. Jamestown became the first permanent English settlement in the Americas. It was also the first English settlement in North America to have slaves.

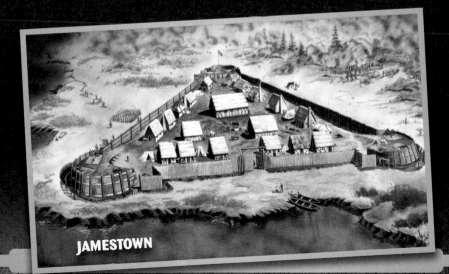

JAMESTOWN

The first African slaves arrived in Jamestown in 1619. A ship landed at Jamestown carrying around 20 Africans. This marked the beginning of slavery in what would become the United States.

The first slaves in Jamestown, such as the ones shown in this image, were treated differently than slaves who came to North America later. Some were even granted their freedom after a set period of time because they were treated like **indentured servants**.

LEAVING AFRICA

The Africans who were forced to **migrate** across the Atlantic Ocean left behind a homeland filled with different **cultures** and traditions. African slaves came from a continent made up of many countries with thousands of different languages. They practiced different religions and had different **customs**.

Slaves in Africa sometimes worked for rulers such as kings. However, many of the Africans forced into slavery in America hadn't been slaves in their homeland. Some were prisoners of war, and some were criminals whose punishment for their crime was a life of slavery. Other Africans forced into slavery were taken from their homes and sold to slave merchants. They never saw their homeland again, but they often tried to hold on to their culture even during their time as slaves.

When slaves were taken from their homes in Africa, they were sometimes chained together and forced to walk long distances to European forts. Many Africans died on these difficult journeys.

THE MIDDLE PASSAGE

Once enslaved Africans reached European forts, they were held there until they were forced onto a slave ship bound for North America or South America. They were herded below deck like cattle, and they often had no idea where they were being taken.

The journey for slaves across the Atlantic Ocean was called the Middle Passage. During their time on the ship, they were chained together and given little to eat. Sometimes they were packed so tightly some of them **suffocated**.

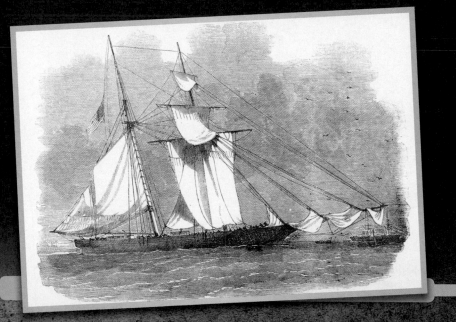

There were no bathrooms, and many of the slaves became sick. Those who were sick were sometimes thrown overboard to keep sicknesses from spreading. African men, women, and children were all subjected to these terrible conditions. They were treated like animals because they were seen as property and not as people.

The Middle Passage got its name because it was the middle stage of the triangular trade route that brought European goods to Africa, African slaves to America, and American raw materials to Europe.

SOLD AND SEPARATED

If the enslaved Africans survived the Middle Passage, they were sold upon landing on the eastern coast of what would become the United States. Slave dealers or agents bought the slaves from incoming slave ships. Slaves were sold at a fixed price, or people could bargain on the price of a slave. Slave auctions were often held to sell slaves to the highest bidder.

The men, women, and children sold into slavery were poked and examined roughly by slave dealers. They were often tired and confused after weeks of being held captive on ships. After the slaves were sold, the dealers forced them to migrate again—this time to the inland farms and plantations where they would be working.

When slaves were sold directly to individuals or at auctions, they were often separated from any family or friends who made the journey across the Atlantic Ocean with them.

PLANTATION LIFE

African slaves were often sent to work in the southern British colonies. Those colonies had many huge plantations that greatly benefited from the free labor of slaves. Slavery also existed in farming regions farther north, such as areas of colonial New York and New Jersey.

Once sold, slaves were often branded with a hot iron to identify them if they tried to escape. Many slaves on plantations were forced to work in the fields from dawn until dusk, taking orders from a **supervisor**. They weren't paid, and they were beaten if the work wasn't done properly. Other slaves worked in their owner's house or barn. These slaves didn't have to work in the hot sun like slaves in the fields, but they still worked without pay and faced harsh treatment such as beatings.

This image shows slaves working in the fields on a plantation. A supervisor is also shown here holding a whip, which was used to beat slaves.

15

SEARCHING FOR COMFORT

Slaves were seen as property, which made many slave owners feel as if they could treat slaves as less than human. Owners could treat their slaves as they pleased, which meant they could beat or even kill them without being punished.

Slaves weren't allowed to decide where they wanted to live or what they wanted to do. They could be sold at any time to another owner. Even if a family had stayed together for a long time, they could still be suddenly separated.

There was very little comfort in a slave's life. However, slaves did find some comfort in religion and in the company of the other slaves. Their shared beliefs and shared sorrows helped them feel less alone.

One of the ways people learned about the terrible treatment slaves endured was by reading slave narratives, or first-person accounts of a slave's life. Frederick Douglass and Harriet Jacobs were two former slaves who wrote narratives that showed people the truth about how slaves were treated.

FREDERICK DOUGLASS

HARRIET JACOBS

THE GROWTH OF SLAVERY

Slavery wasn't legalized in all 13 British colonies in North America at once. Massachusetts was the first colony to legalize slavery in 1641. In the next few years, Connecticut and Virginia also legally recognized slavery. By 1750, all 13 colonies had legalized slavery.

The number of slaves brought from Africa to European colonies in America increased partly because of a law that was passed in 1689 by the British Parliament, or lawmaking body. It stated that any British subject could trade in slaves. The number of slaves being transported on British ships jumped from 5,000 slaves per year in the late 1600s to 45,000 slaves per year by the middle of the next century. Slavery continued to grow in North America even as Americans began fighting for their freedom from the British.

Slavery grew in North America as crops such as cotton became more important to southern economies. As more cotton was produced, more slaves were needed to pick and clean the cotton.

A NEW CULTURE

As time passed, new generations of slaves were born in America rather than migrating from Africa. As the separation between them and their homeland grew, they began to adopt parts of American culture. Some slaves began to accept Christianity as their religion, finding comfort in the Bible and its message of freedom and equality.

Slaves still found some ways to hold on to their African **heritage**, though. Music was one way in which slaves could keep a sense of themselves, in spite of the mistreatment they suffered. Blues and jazz music heard today are examples of music with African roots. Music and religion were deeply connected in slaves' lives, and slaves would often sing spiritual songs to bring them comfort in hard times.

Religion was very important to many slaves and former slaves. Some churches, such as the African Methodist Episcopal (AME) Church, gave a voice to all people, including women. Juliann Jane Tillman was a preacher in the AME church during the nineteenth century.

THE END OF SLAVERY

Slavery had been a topic of moral debate from its earliest days in North America. By the end of the 1700s, these questions of morality were becoming louder and more frequent. There was often conflict in America between those who supported slavery and those who opposed it.

In 1807, Congress took the first step toward outlawing slavery by passing a law that banned the importing of slaves. By 1830, slavery had become an **institution** that was mainly limited to the southern United States.

The conflict over slavery eventually played a major role in the American Civil War. Although slavery was officially abolished, or ended, in 1865, it took many years for African Americans to be granted the same rights as white Americans. The fight for equality was far from over.

GLOSSARY

culture: The beliefs and ways of life of a certain group of people.

custom: An action or way of behaving that is traditional among the people in a certain group or place.

engraving: A print made from a plate into which an artist cut a design.

heritage: The traditions, achievements, and beliefs that are part of the history of a group or nation.

immigrant: A person who comes to a country to live there.

indentured servant: A person who is bound to work for another for a specific period of time, often in exchange for passage to a new country.

institution: A custom, practice, or law that is accepted and used by many people.

migrate: To move from one place to settle in another.

suffocate: To die because you are unable to breathe.

supervisor: A person who watches and directs someone or something.

INDEX

PRIMARY SOURCE LIST

Page 17. *Frederick Douglass.* Created by Frank W. Legg. ca. 1879. Photograph. Now kept at the National Archives at College Park, College Park, MD.

Page 21. *Mrs. Juliann Jane Tillman, Preacher of the A.M.E. Church.* Created by Alfred M. Hoffy and printed by Peter S. Duval. Lithograph. ca. 1844. Now kept at the Library of Congress Prints and Photographs Division, Washington, D.C.

WEBSITES

Due to the changing nature of Internet links, PowerKids Press has developed an online list of websites related to the subject of this book. This site is updated regularly. Please use this link to access the list: www.powerkidslinks.com/soim/tst